Portraits of President Donald Trump and the First Family:
an Adult Coloring Book

by

Stephen Jorgensen
(artist)

published by
CyberSuccess Publishing
Honolulu, Hawaii

i

President Donald Trump and the First Family are presented here in the Adult Coloring Book form.

This is a coloring book made for adults. It is not as simple as a child's coloring book because it has smaller and finer details. You have to concentrate when you color to get all the small shapes filled in. The concentration tends to make you clear your mind of thoughts, including many negative thoughts and this will help you relieve your stress. You will find that coloring will tend to reduce anxiety, and will help you focus and in the process it will make you more MINDFULL. It is a therapeutic exercise.

Donald Trump is now the 45th president of the United States. In this Adult coloring book we present "official" portraits of President Trump and the first family. It will be fun to get to know him and his family as you color in the "posed" portraits. A lot of evening gown portraits of the many attractive women in his life are included here. Also we include "imagined" images of Pres. Trump as he might like to think of himself, perhaps as Father of the Country, or a great military leader, or as royalty. The president and the first family is as close to royalty as we get here in America. Anyway, it will be fun coloring in these attractive images.

I was stunned when Donald trump won the election, but I think all Americans should pull together now, and lend their support to the new leaders and give them a chance, as long as they don't go against our constitution. I know many people don't like Trump because he is often a bombastic, egotistic bully, but they should give him a chance.

It's OK to call him on his many faults, but just remember, most of our leaders were egotists and often not very likable in their own way. It is the nature of politics. Nice guys don't keep pushing to the top of the

olitical world. So I have included hidden symbols or "Easter Eggs" in
ach picture. These remind us of Trump and his family member's short-
omings. Have fun coloring and searching out the Easter eggs and their
eanings.

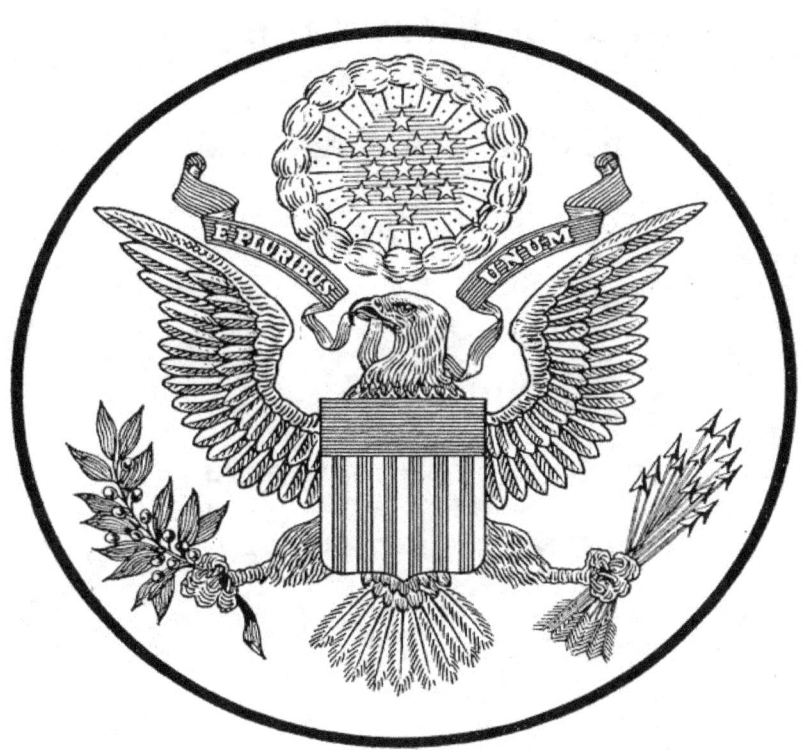

Portraits of President Donald Trump and the First Family:

an Adult Coloring Book

ISBN-13: 978-1542883474

ISBN-10: 1542883474

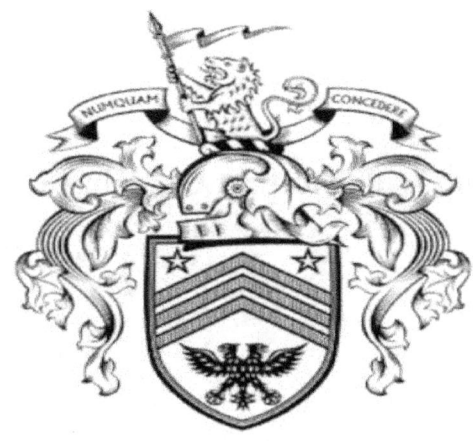

Most of the portraits will require shading of the skin colors and perhaps the clothes to look nice. You can look at the full color reproductions shown on the front and the back covers to see what the shading should look like. You don't have to use the exact same colors for the clothing, try different colors. It helps to "layer" two different colors to get a better color match. For instance, coloring a brown or yellow over a pinkish skin color will give more realistic shading.

There will be no bleed-through to mess up a drawing on the opposite side of the page even if you use color marking pens because the coloring pages are printed on one side only.

Enjoy your coloring.

**You will find that Coloring Therapy
can relax you.**

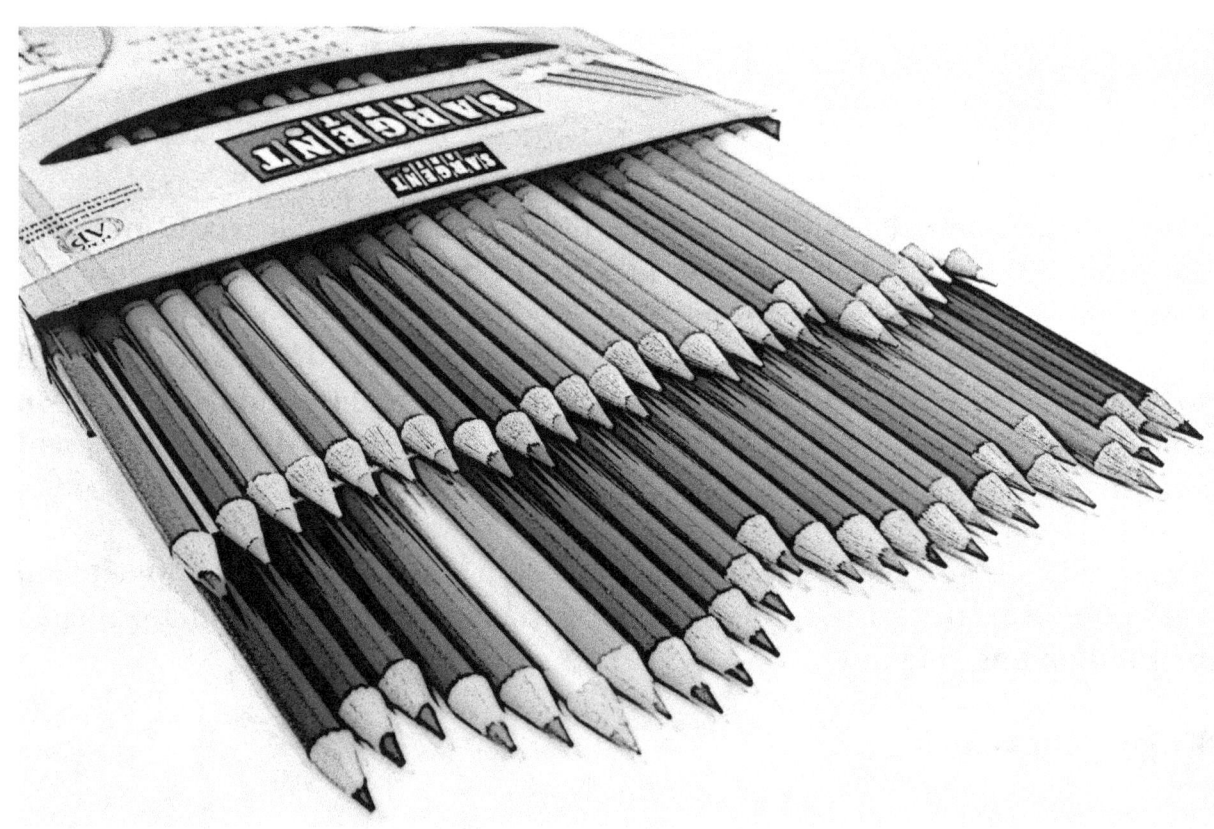

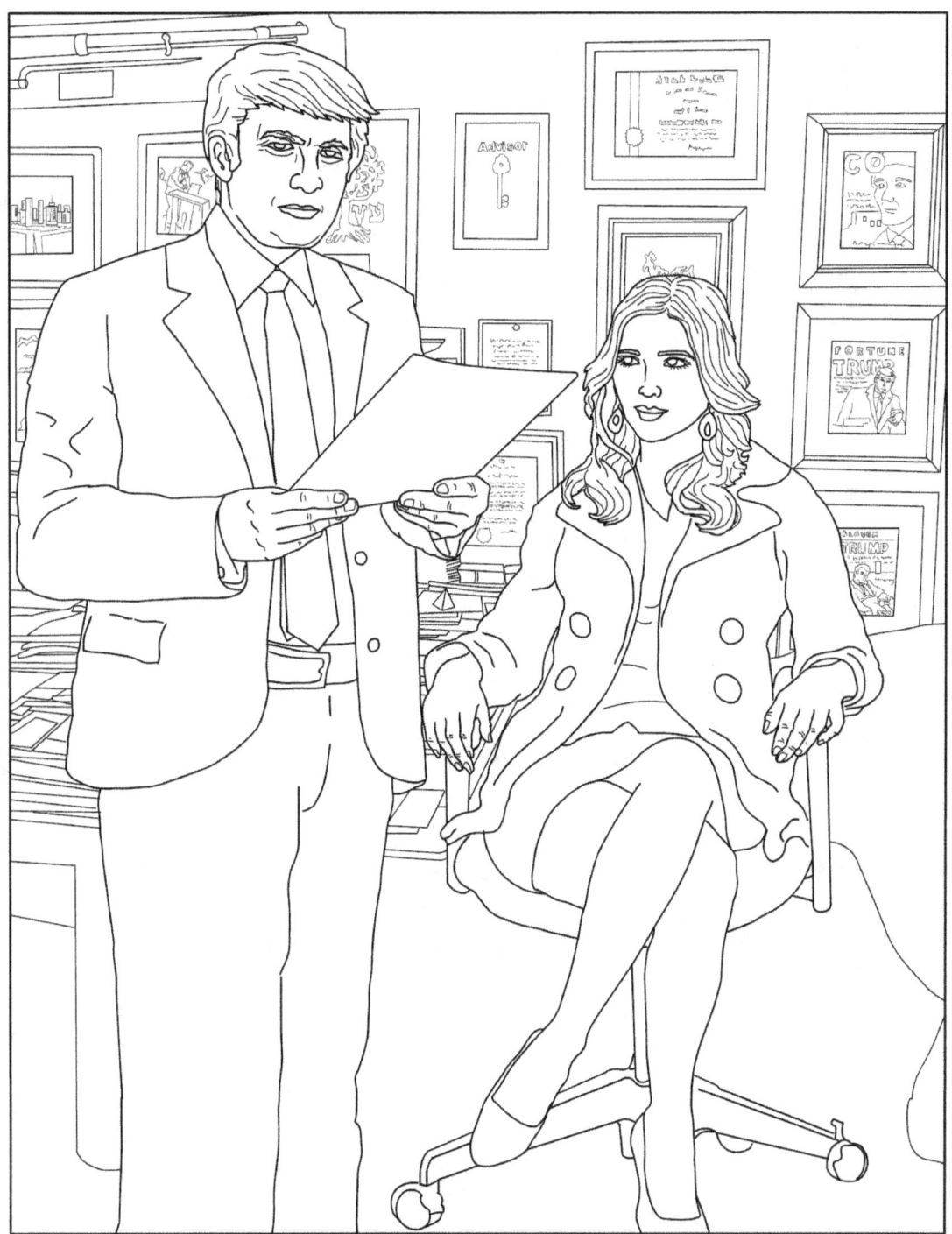

Ivanka with her Father in his office

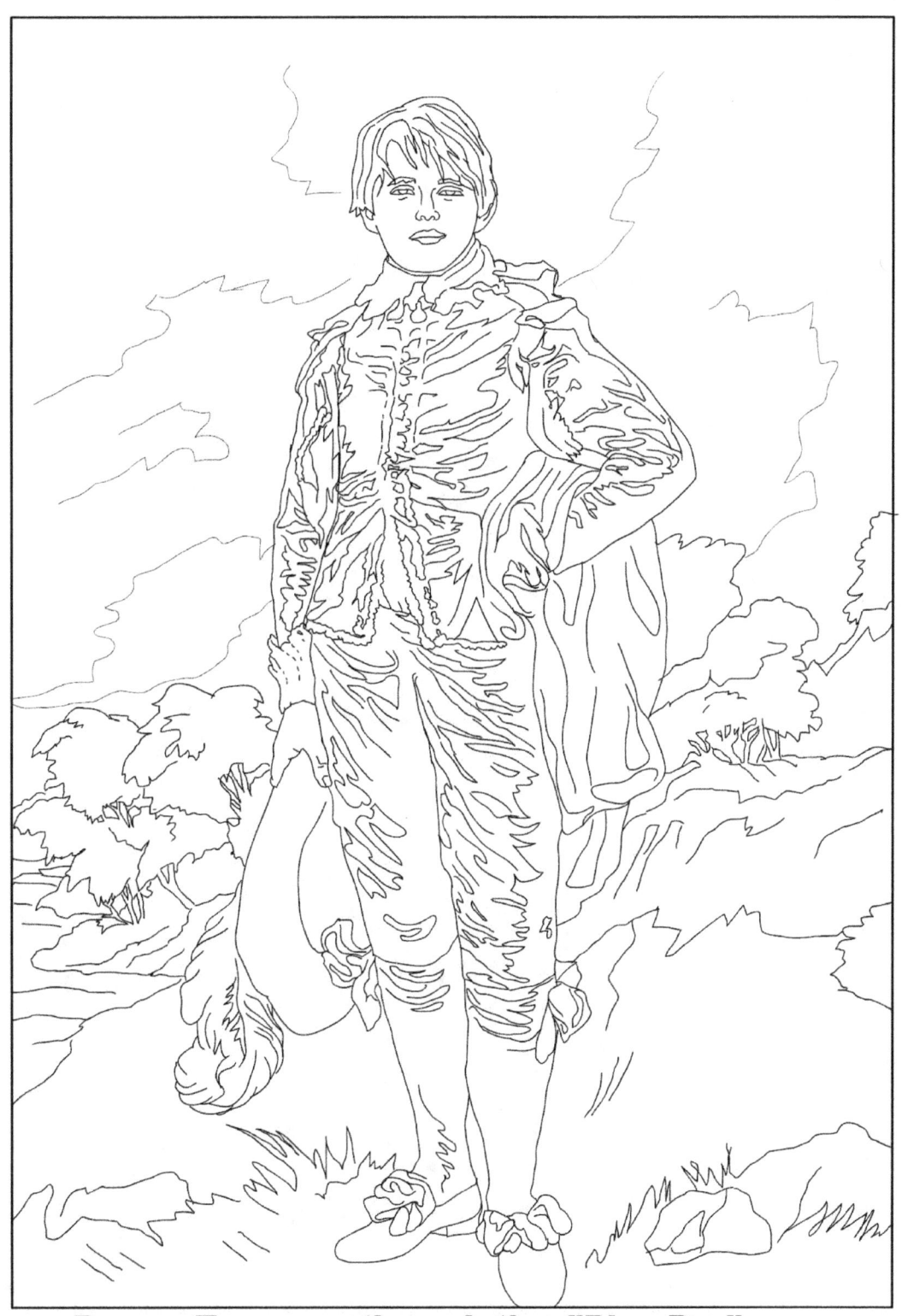

Barron Trump as the painting "Blue Boy"

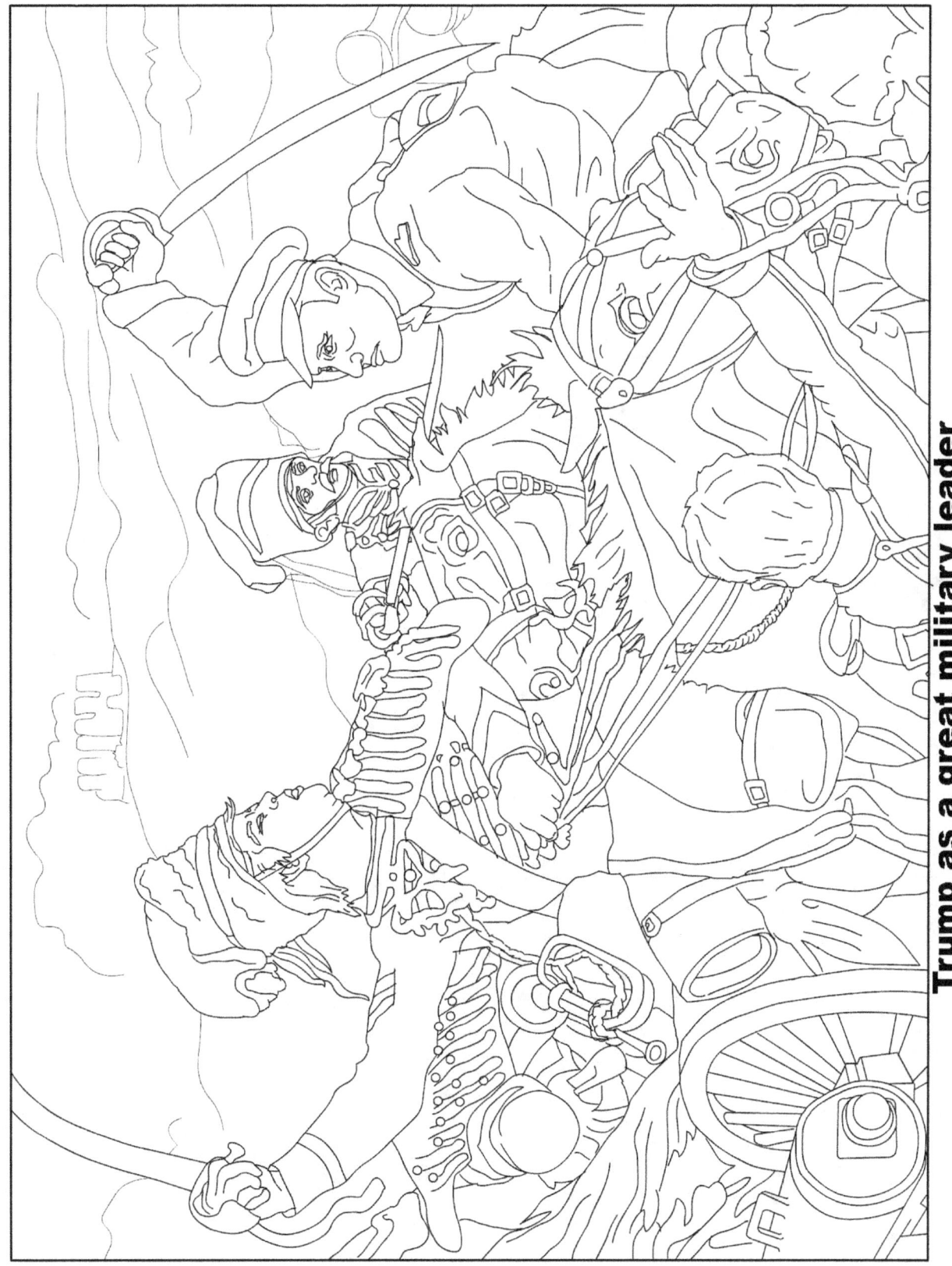

Trump as a great military leader

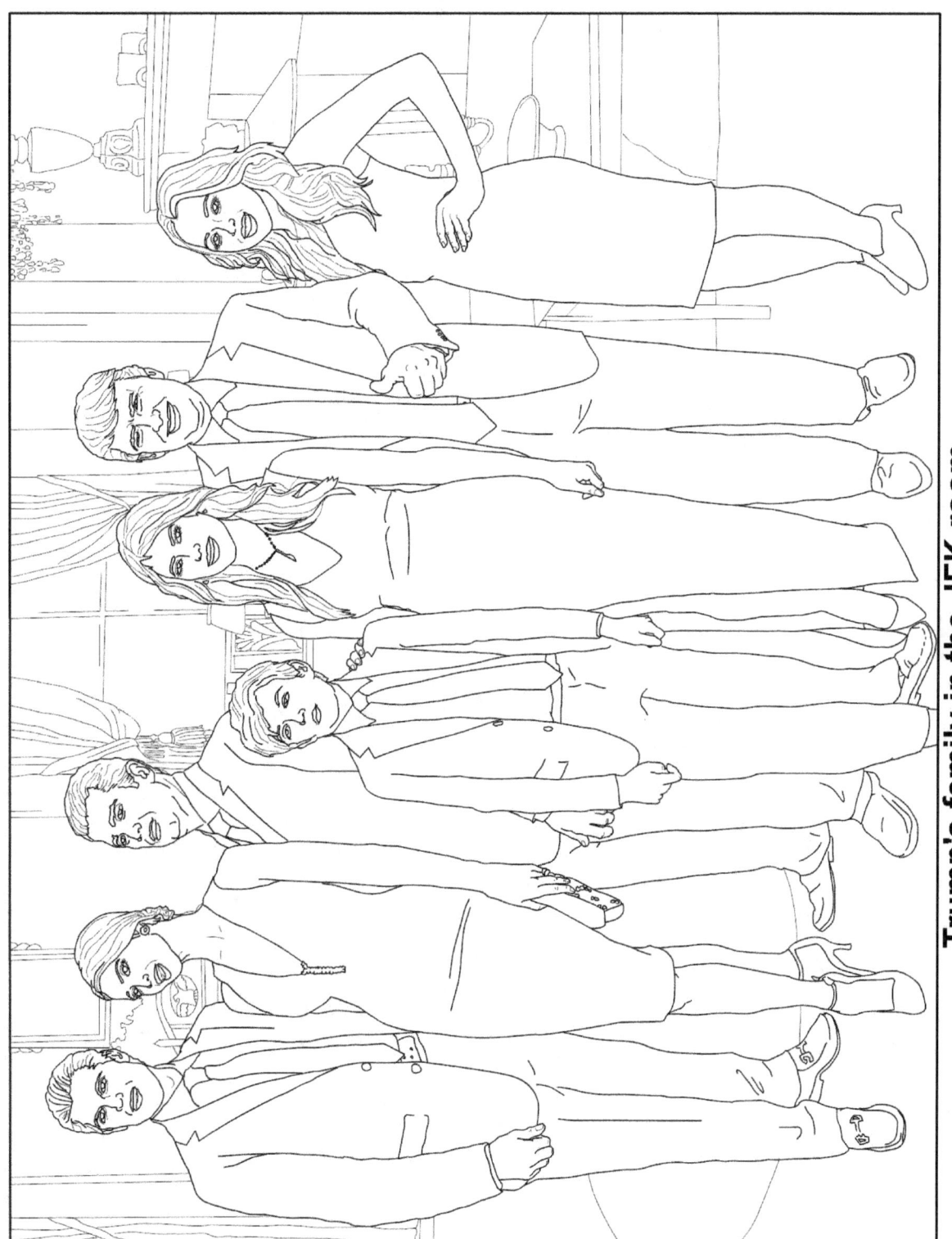

Trump's family in the JFK room

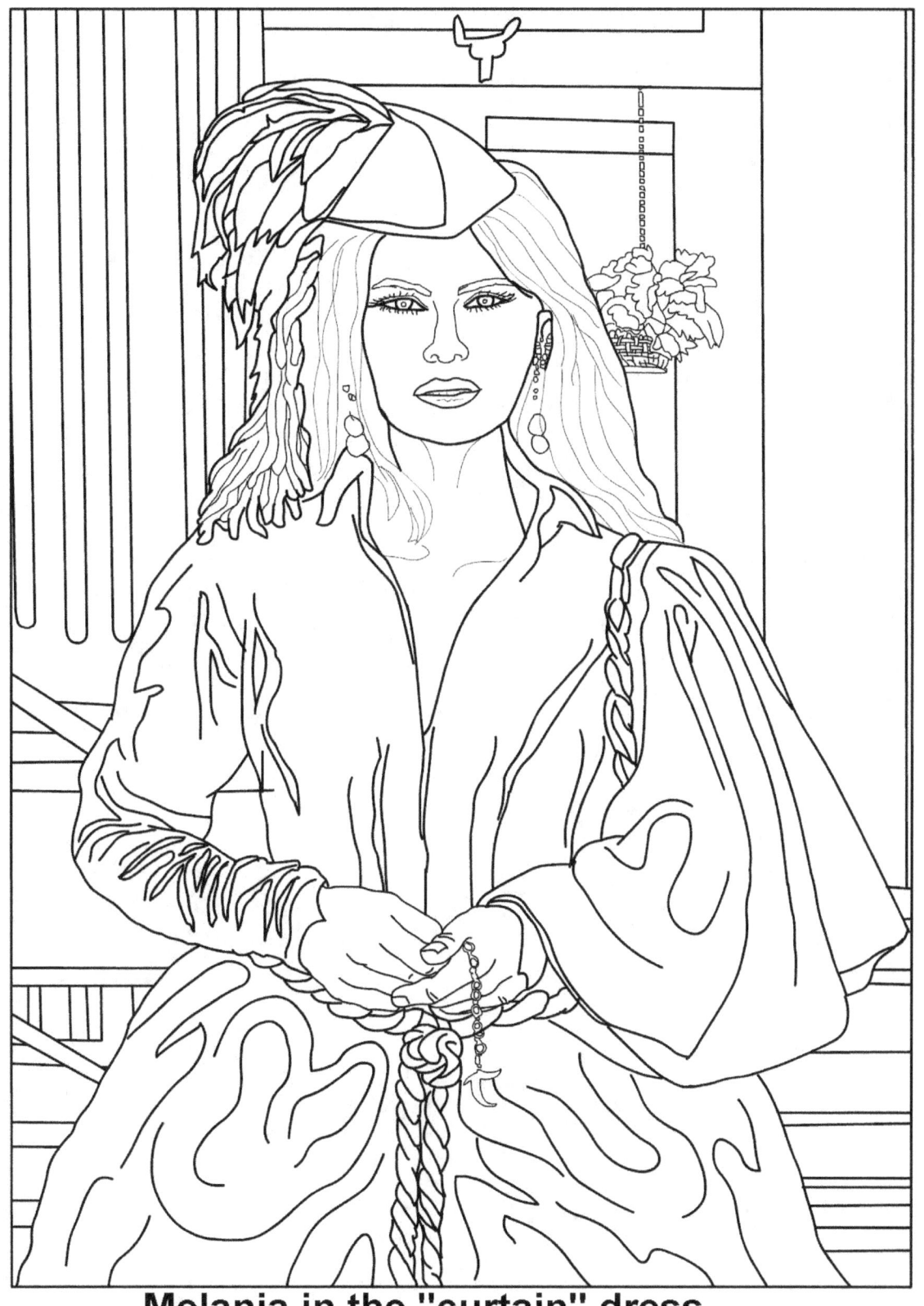

Melania in the "curtain" dress

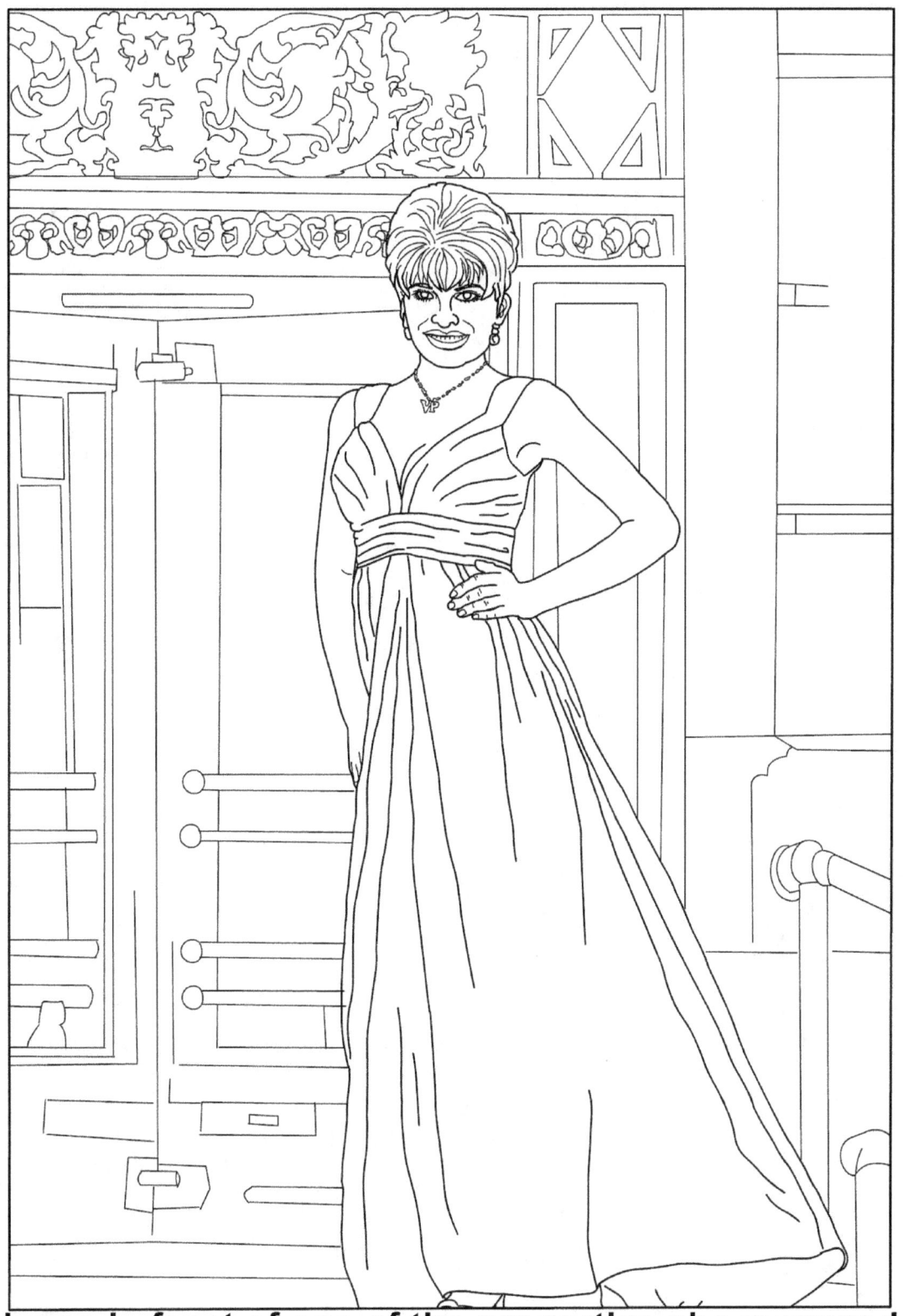

Ivana in front of one of the properties she managed

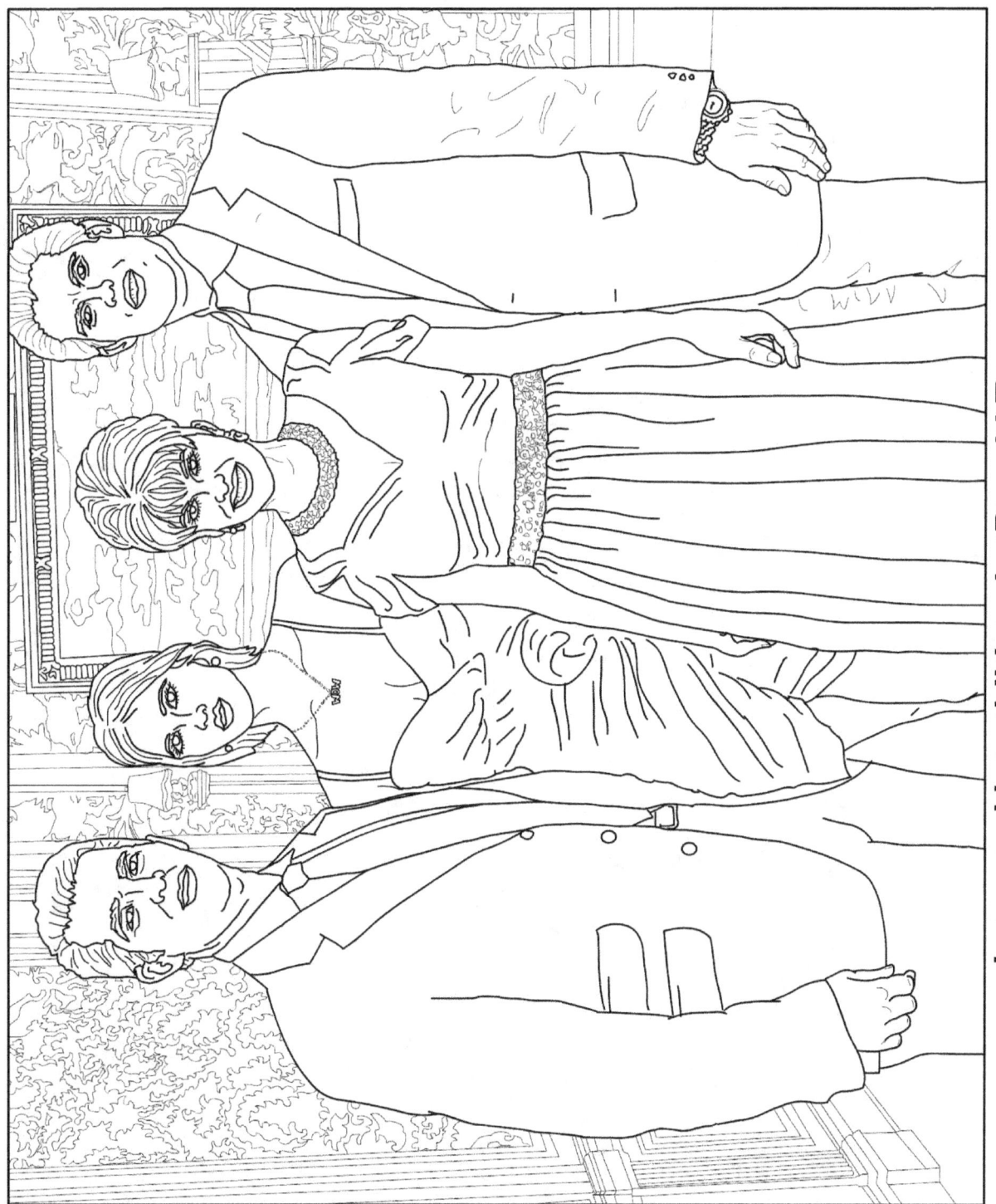

Ivana and her children by Donald Trump

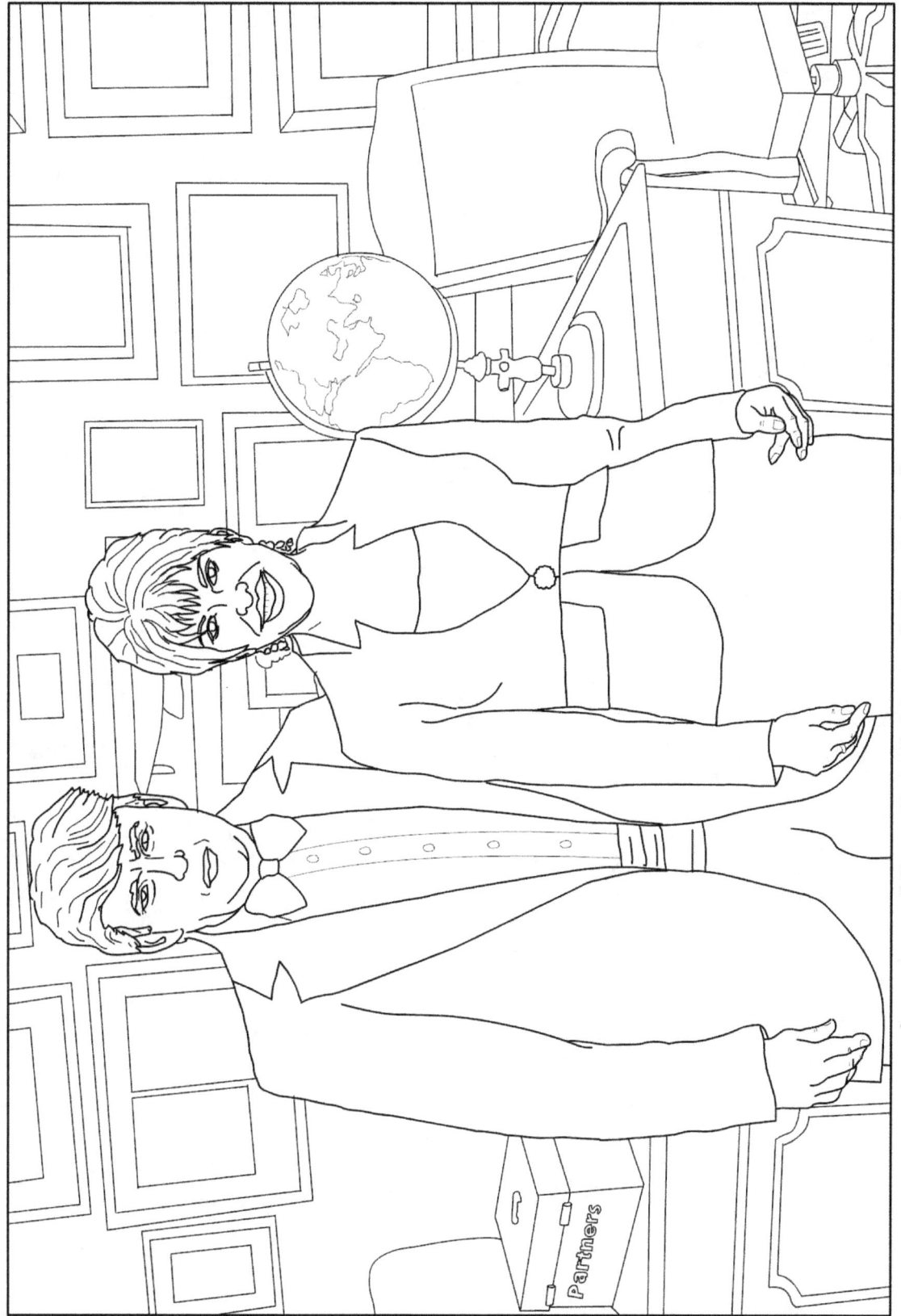

Ivana as Vice-President of Trump's Company

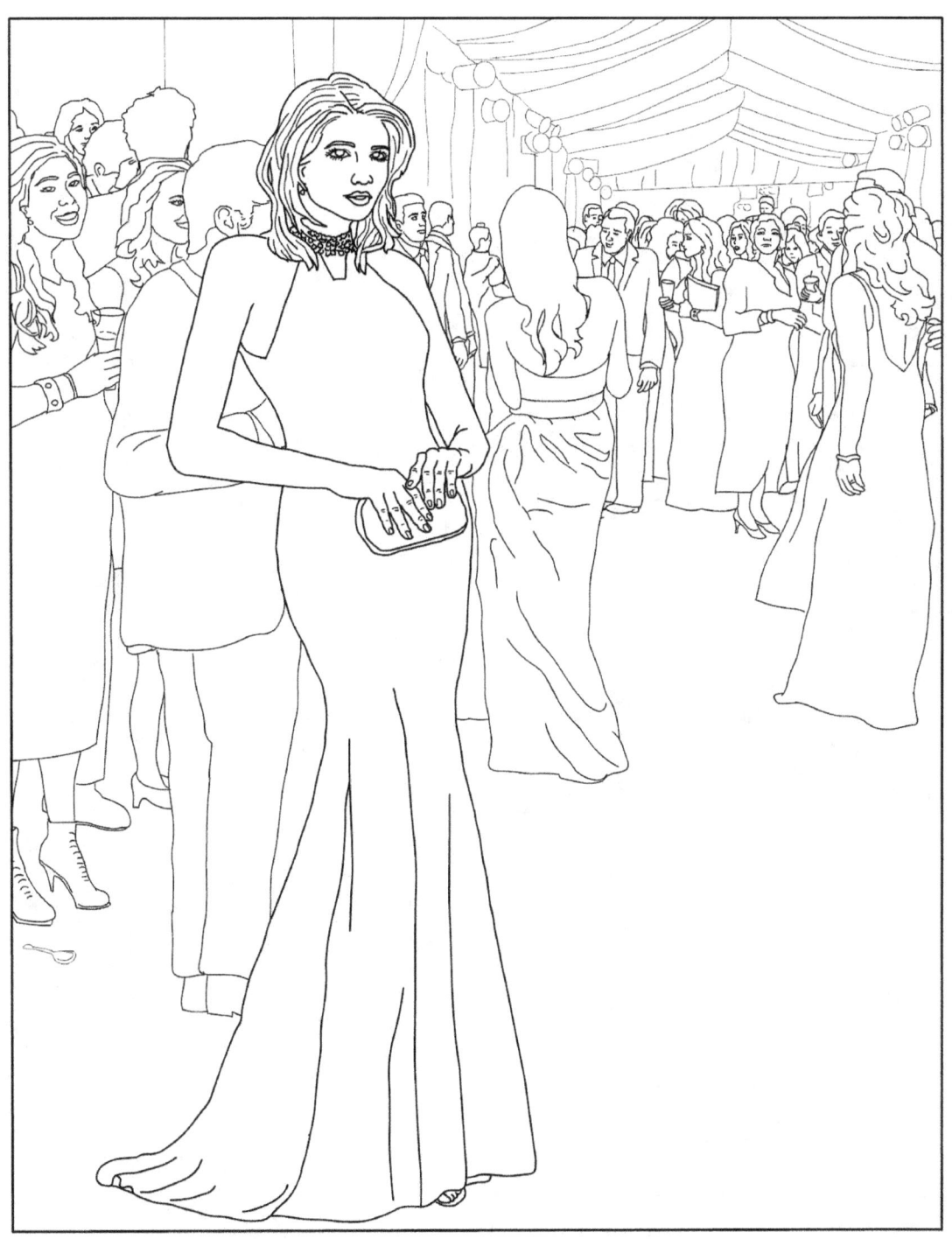

Ivanka at an Inaugural Ball

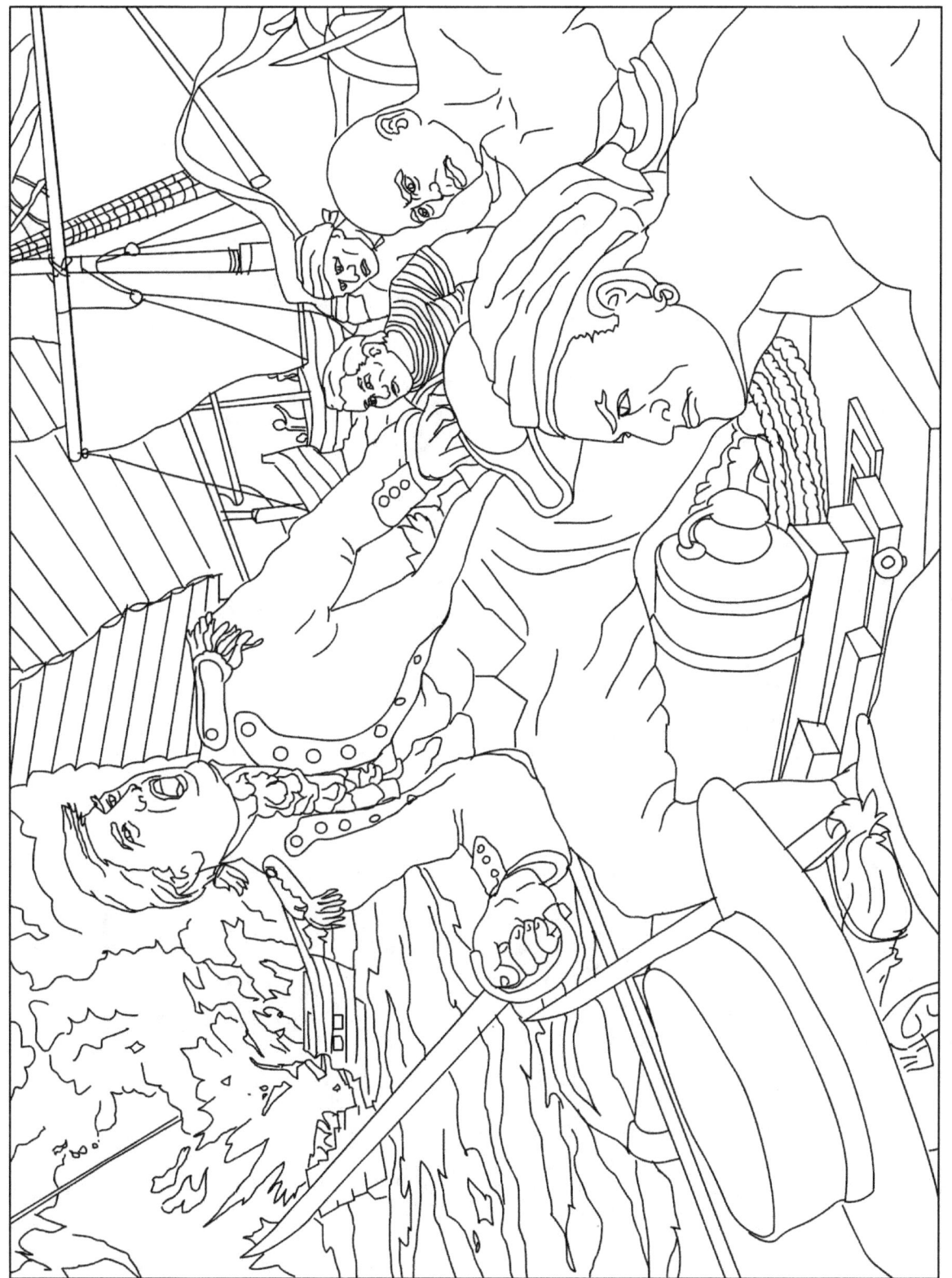

Trump as an old-time naval commander

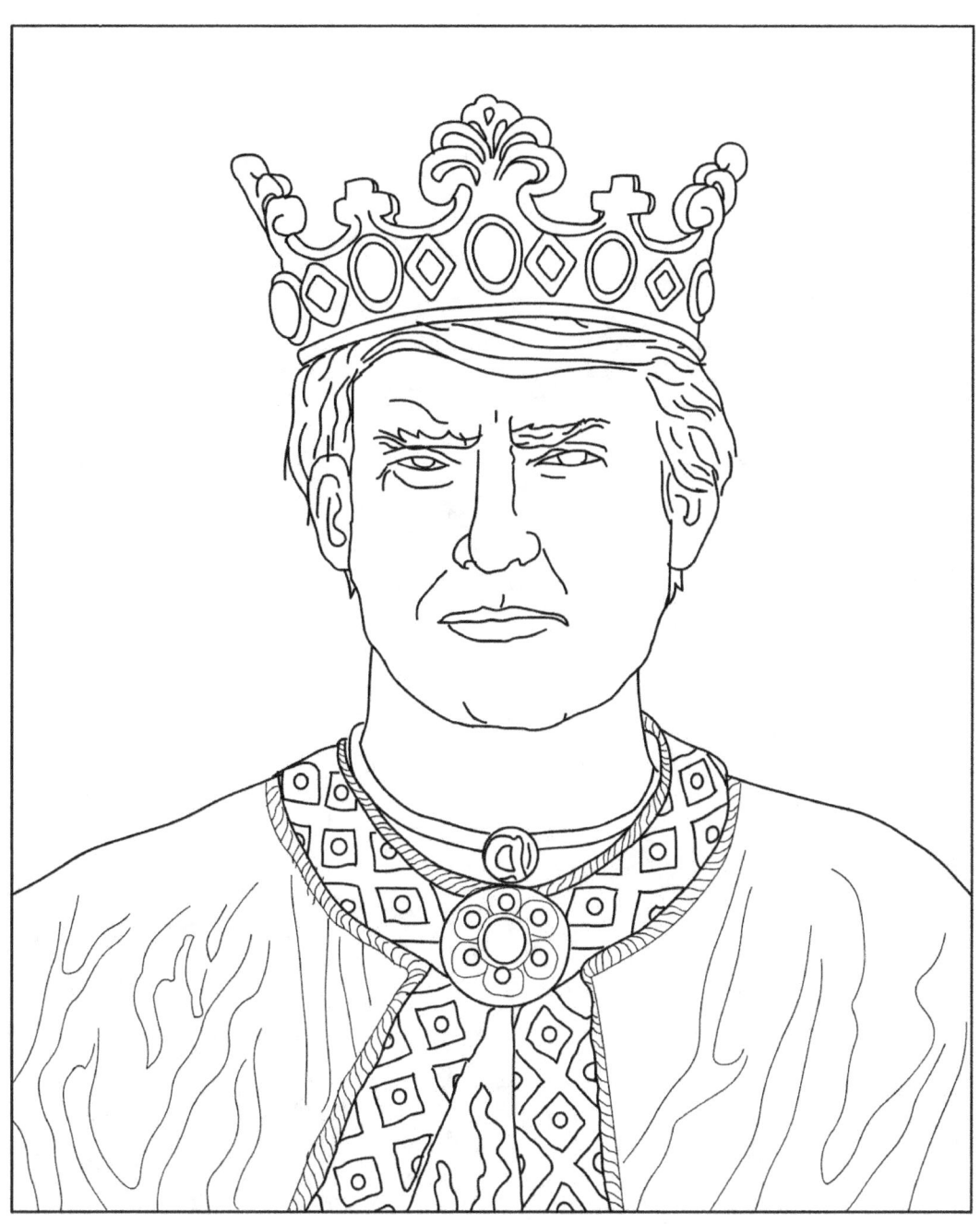

Trump as royalty

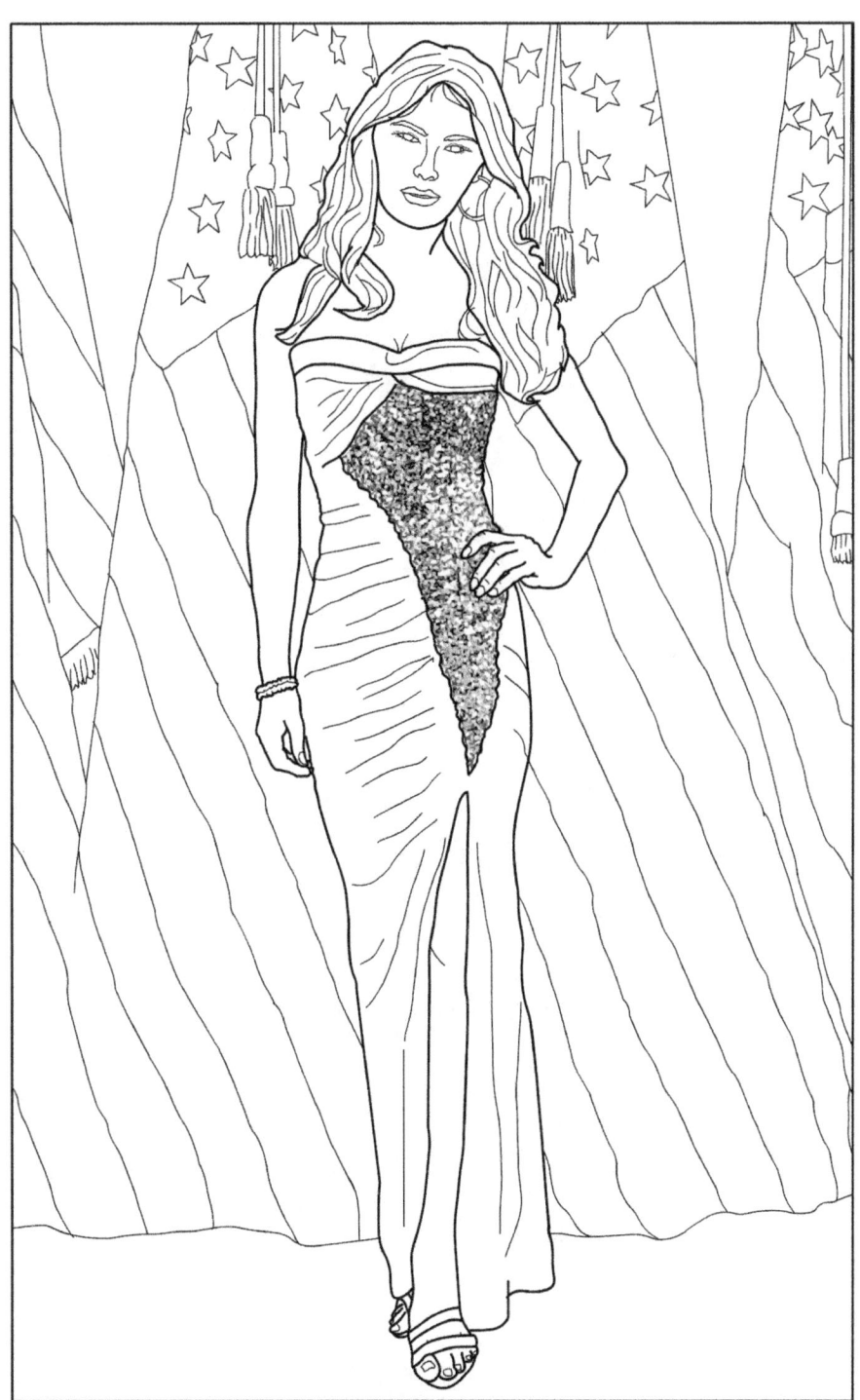

Melania in evening gown

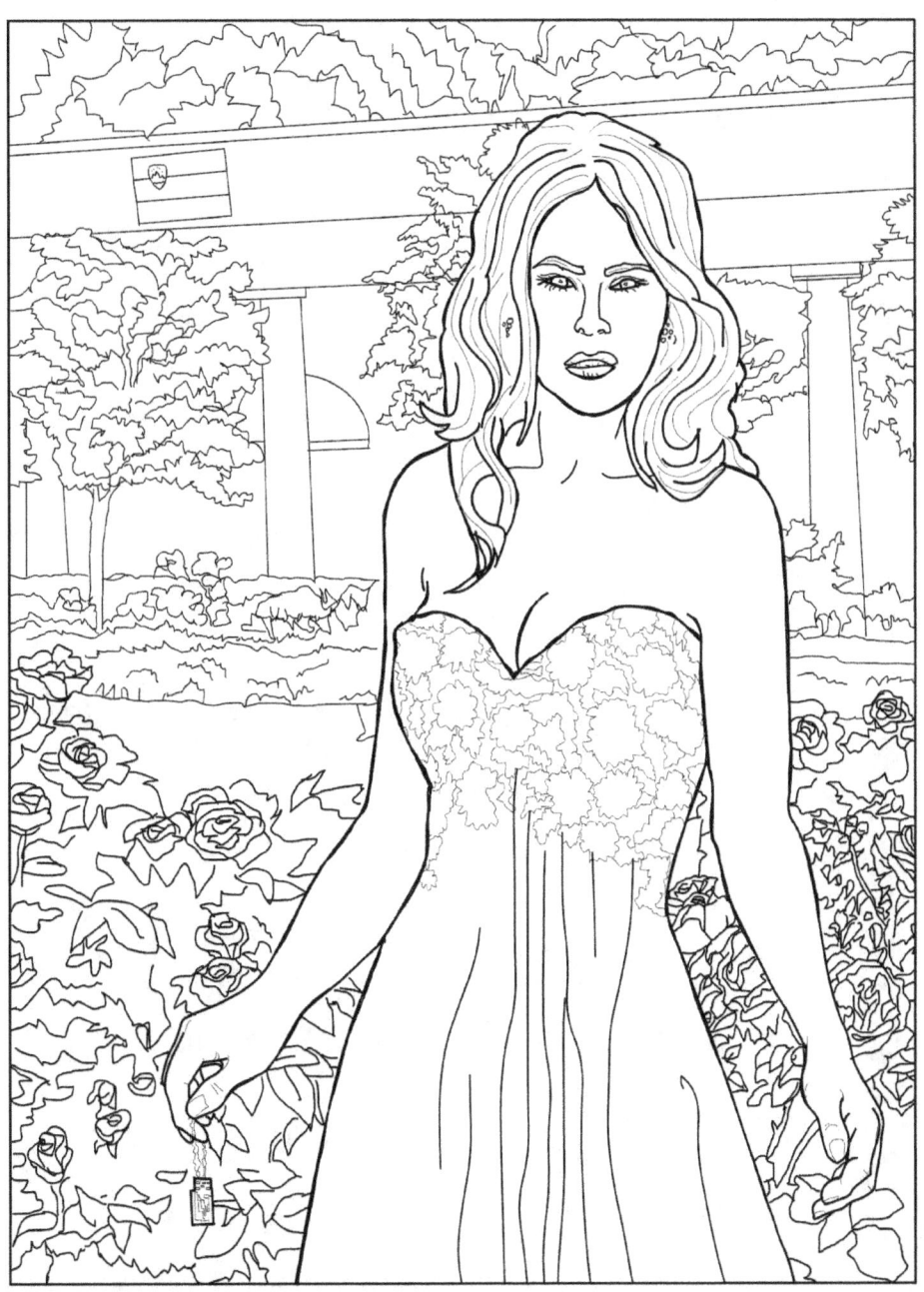

Melania in the White House Rose Garden

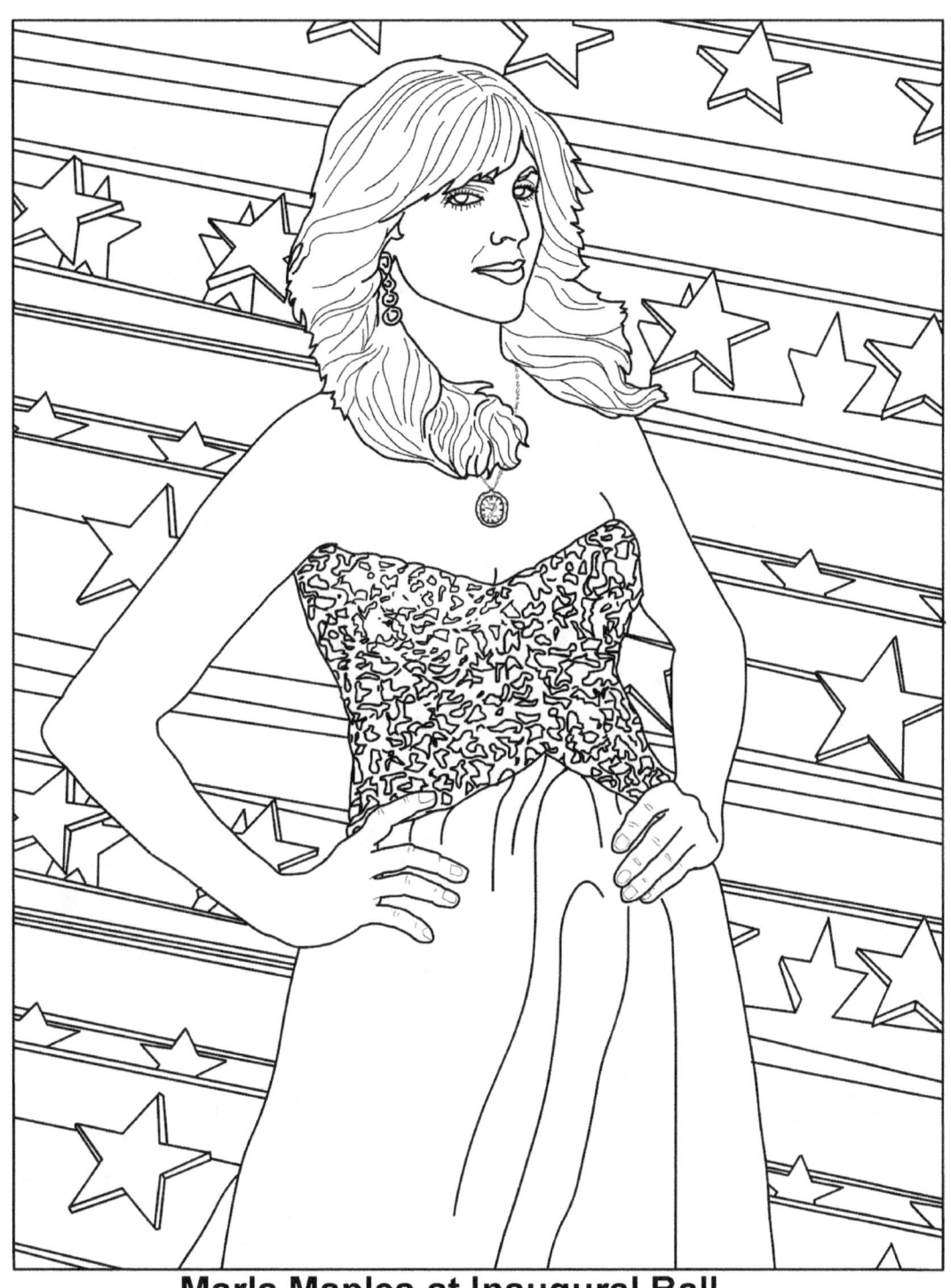

Marla Maples at Inaugural Ball

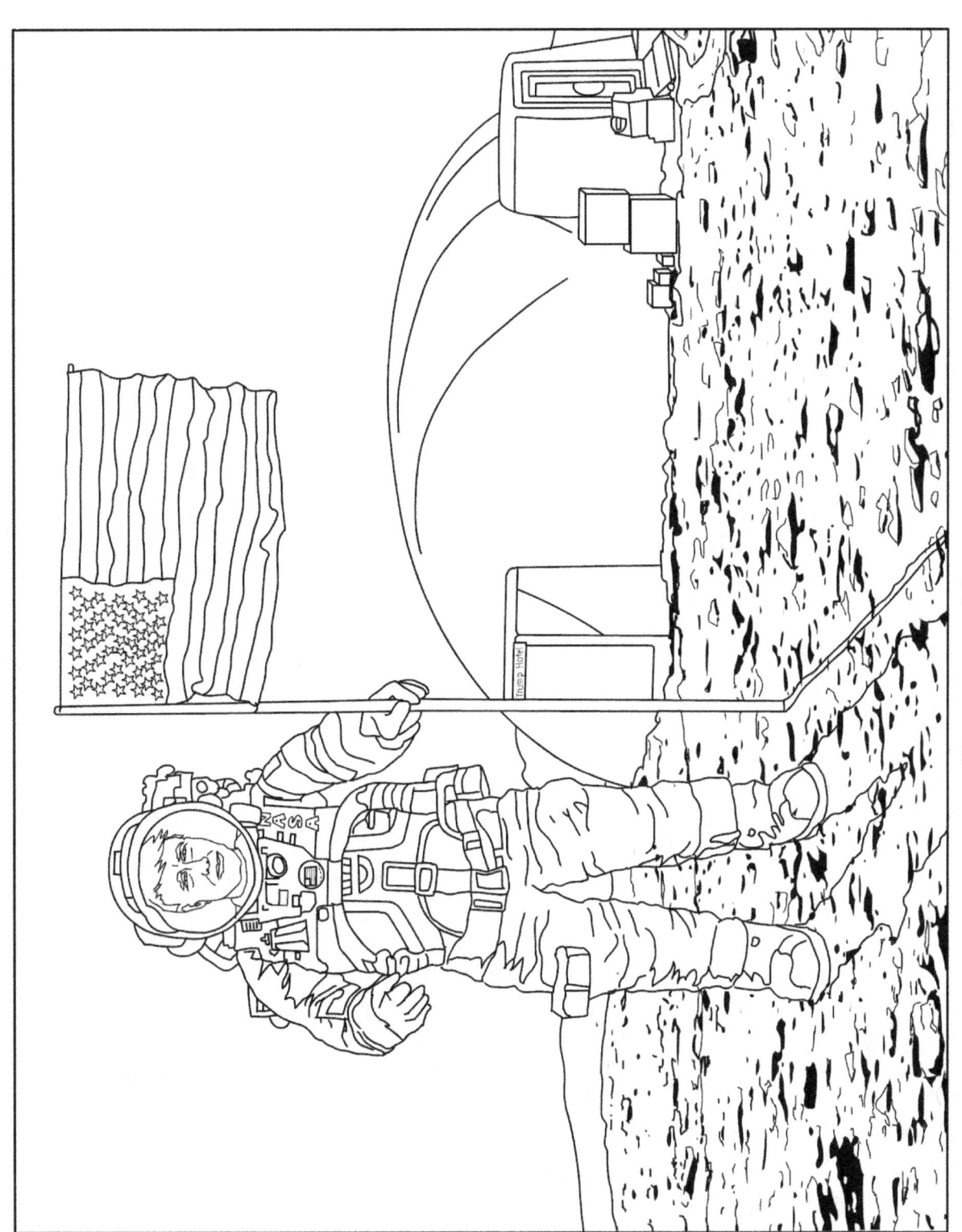

Trump on Mars

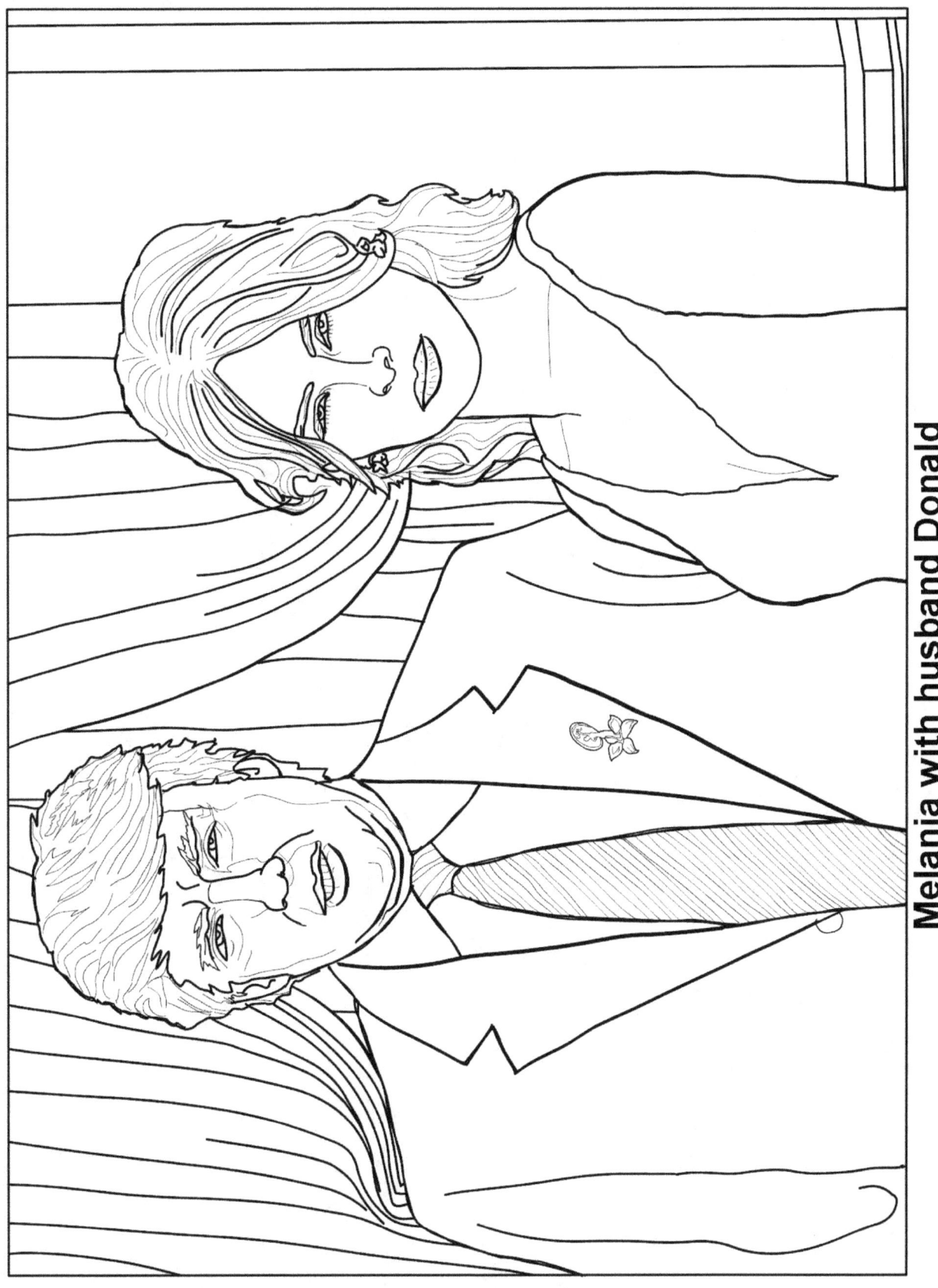

Melania with husband Donald

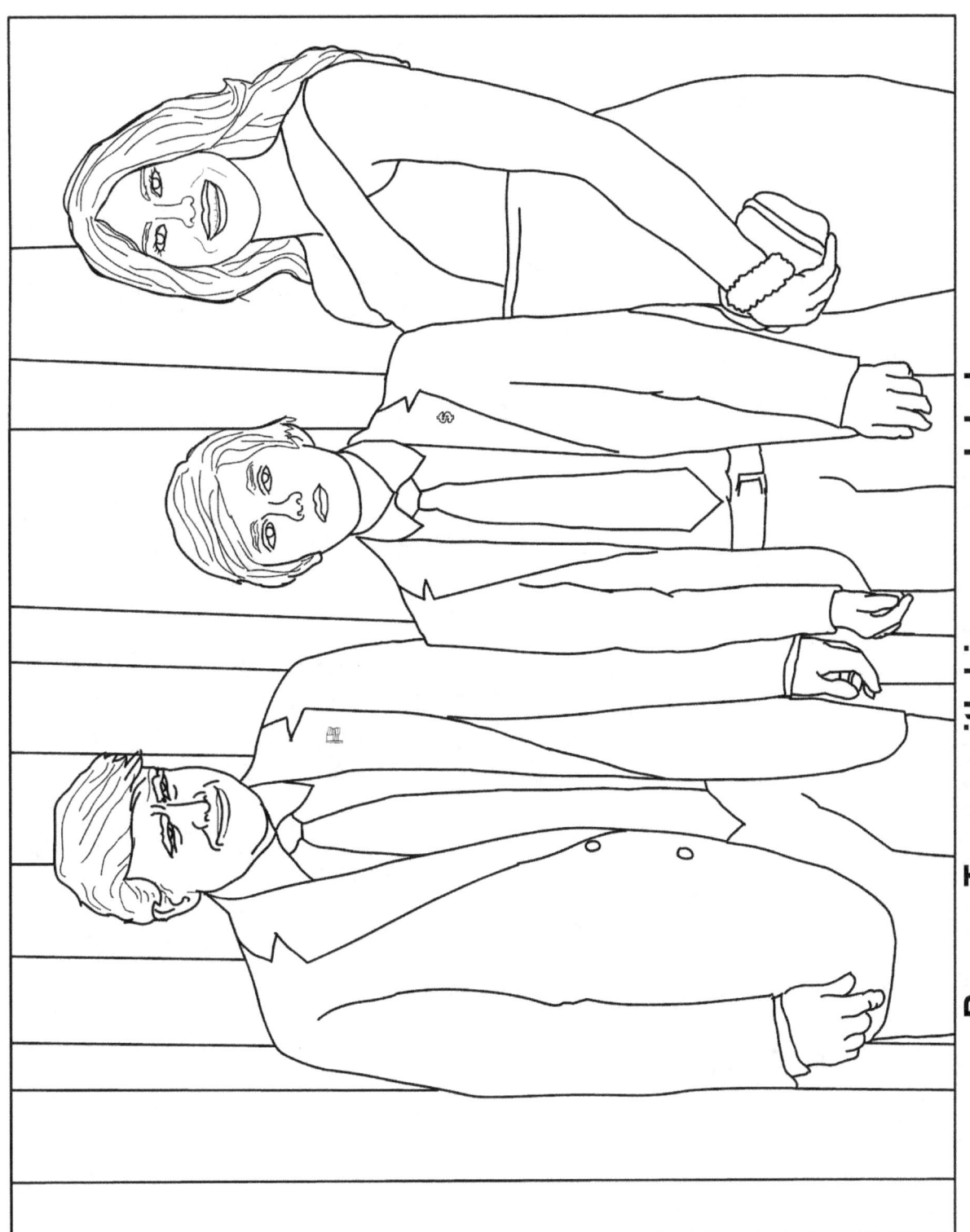

Barron Trump with his mom and dad

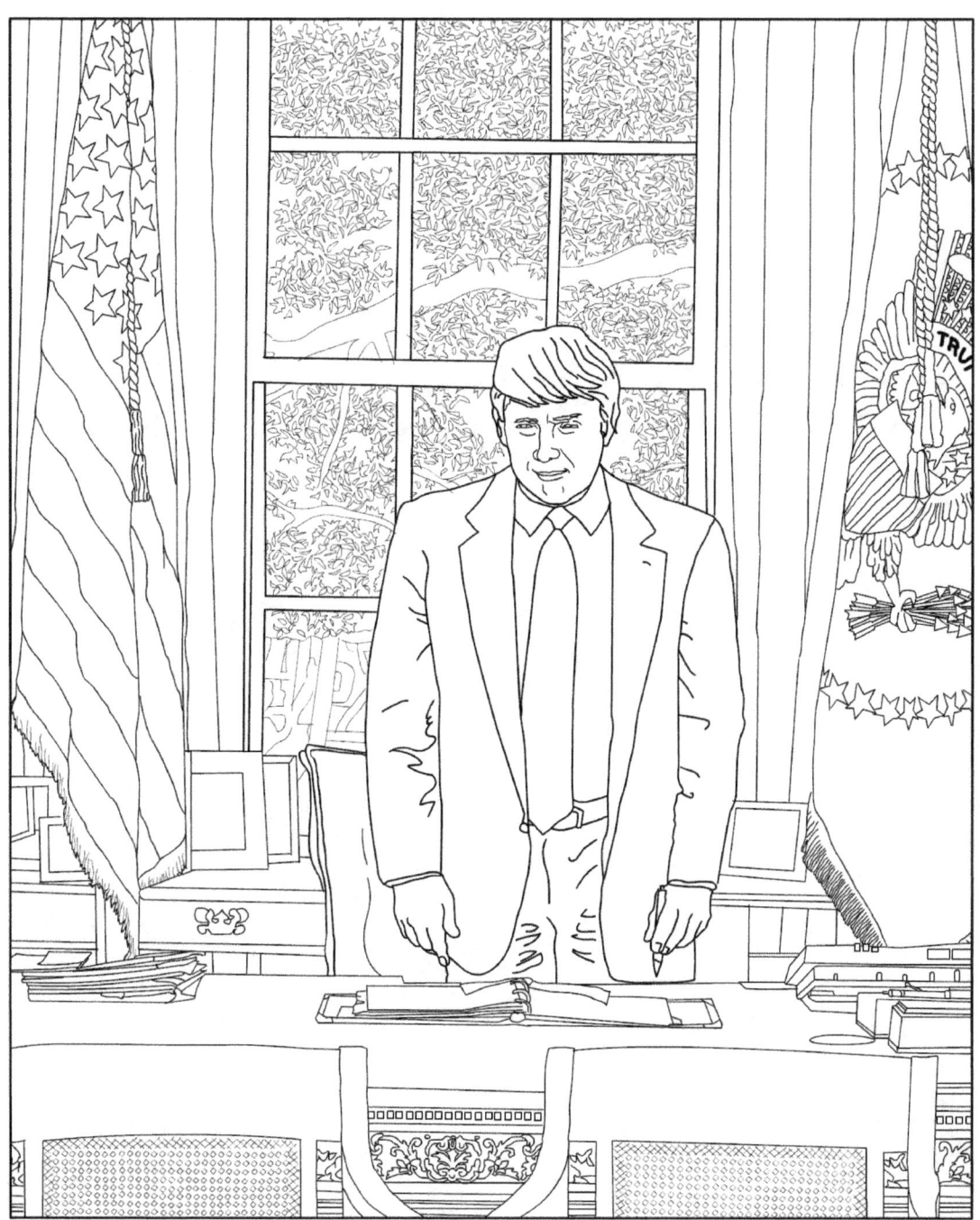

Trump in Oval office

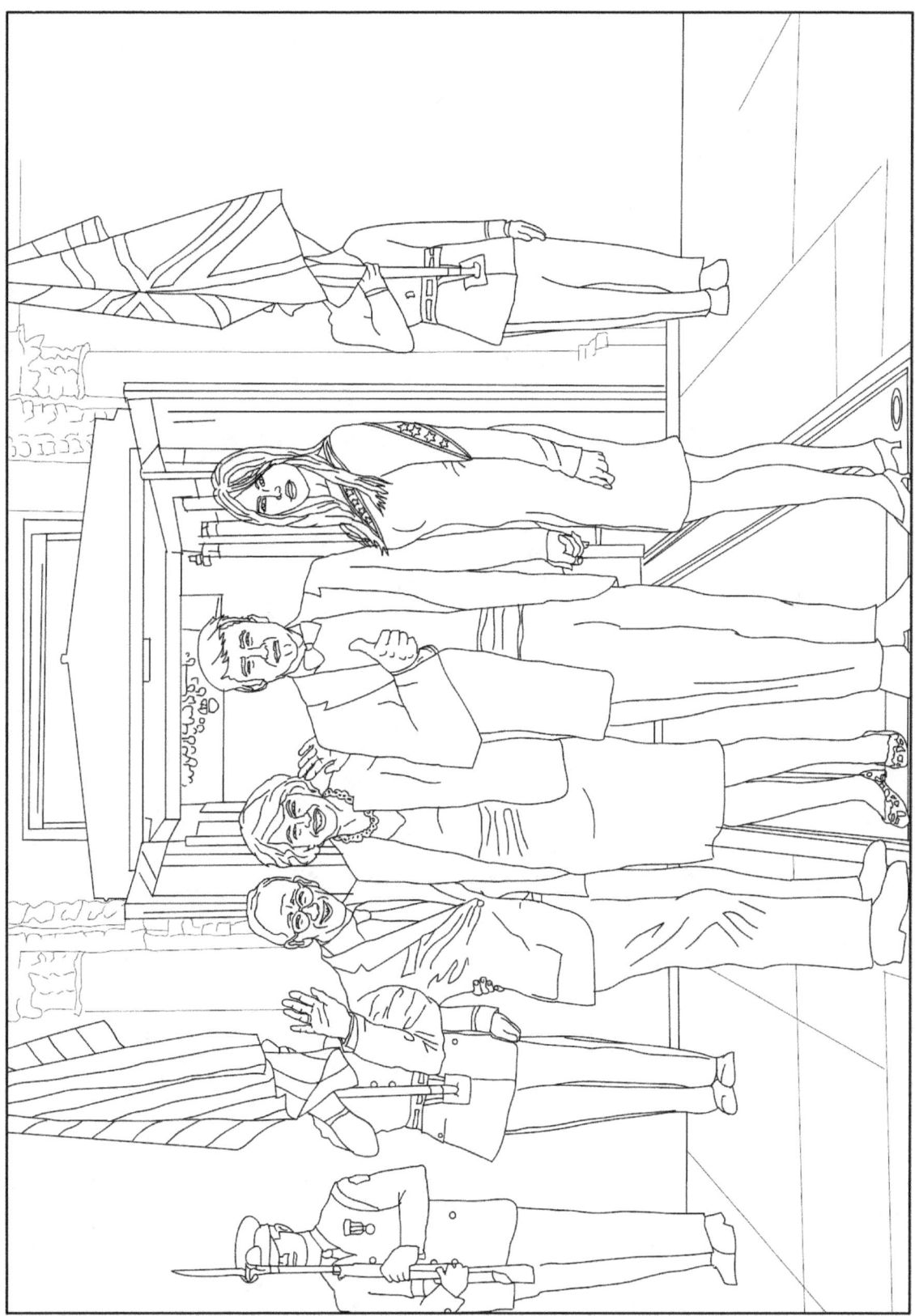

Theresa May and hubby with Trump and Melania

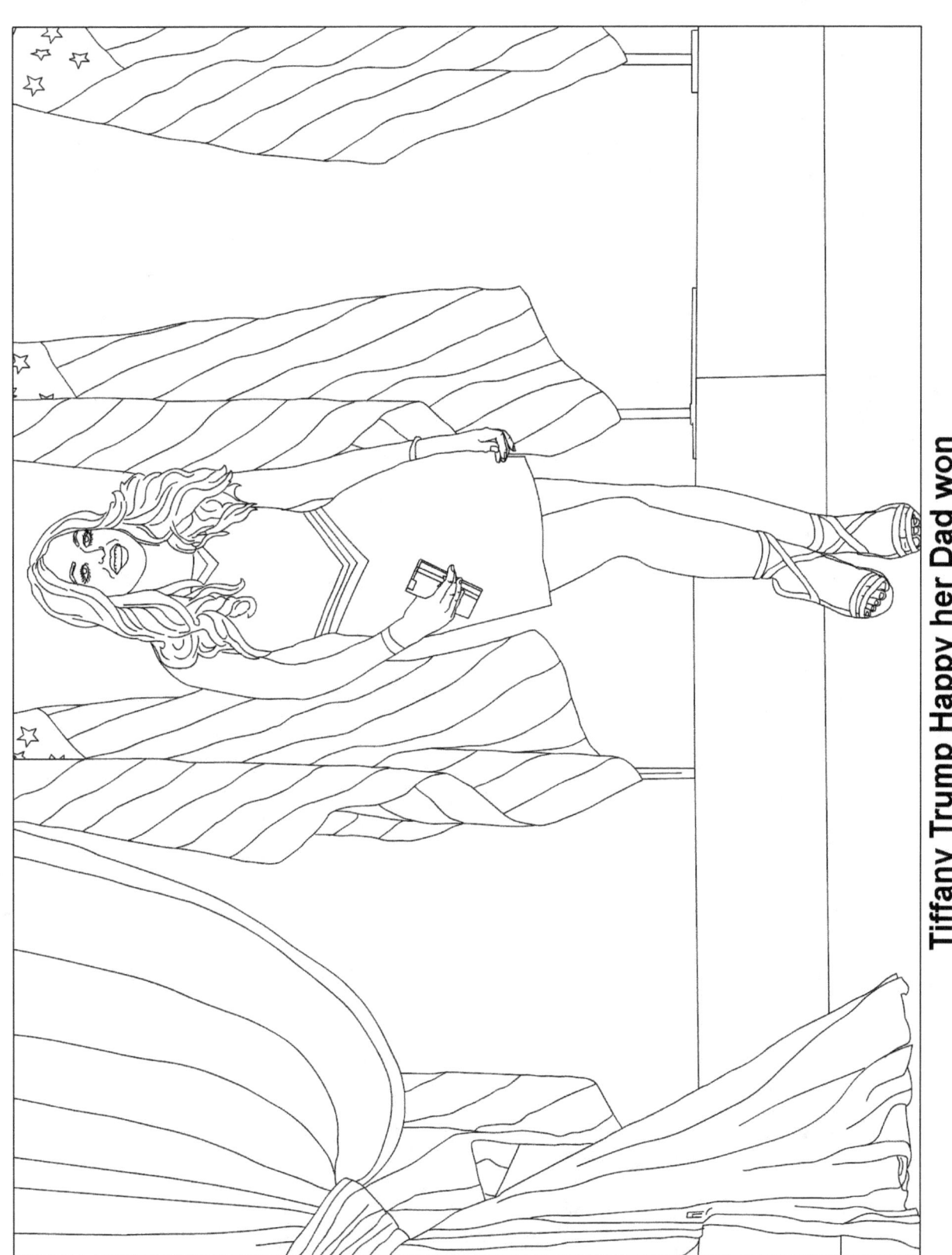

Tiffany Trump Happy her Dad won

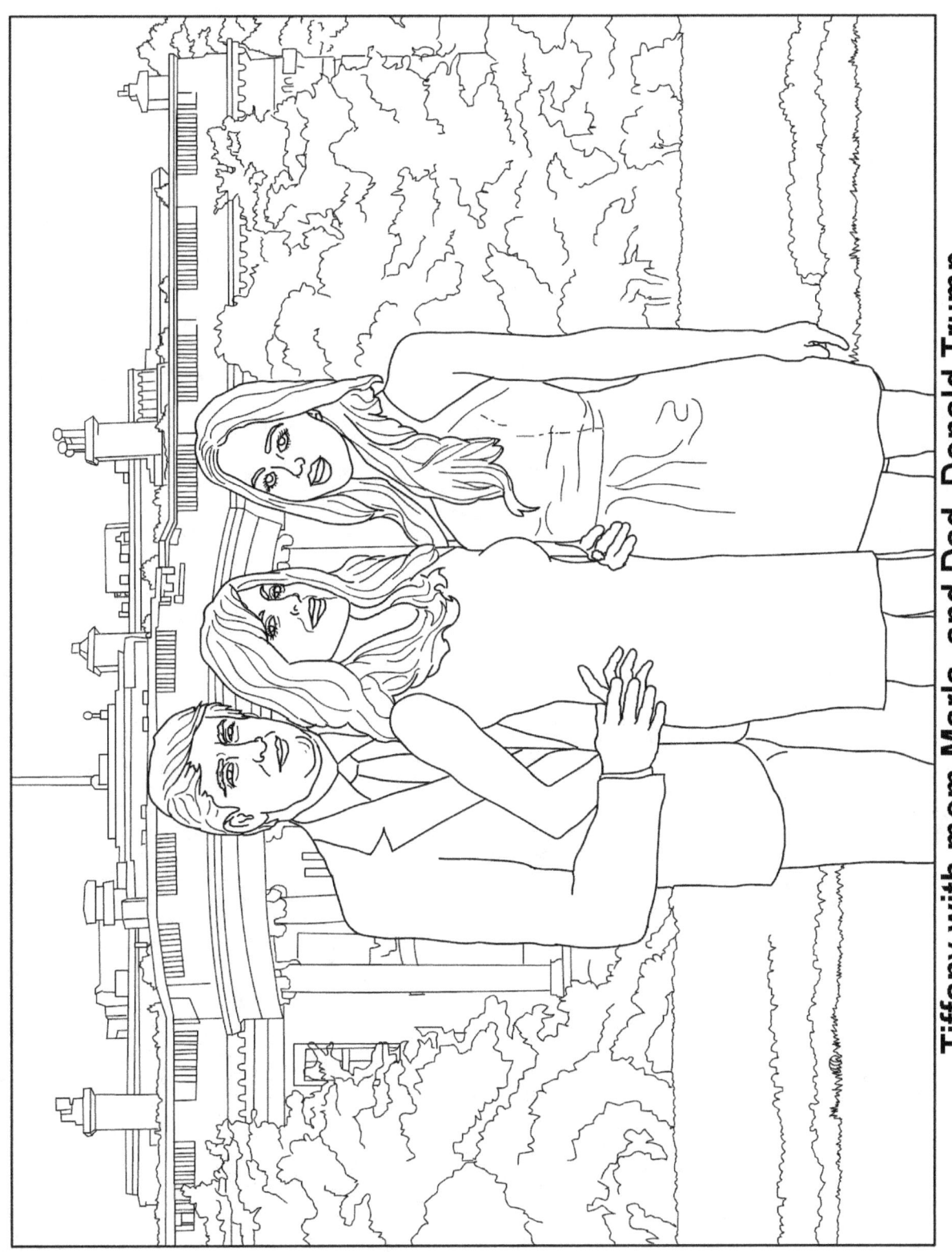

Tiffany with mom Marla, and Dad, Donald Trump

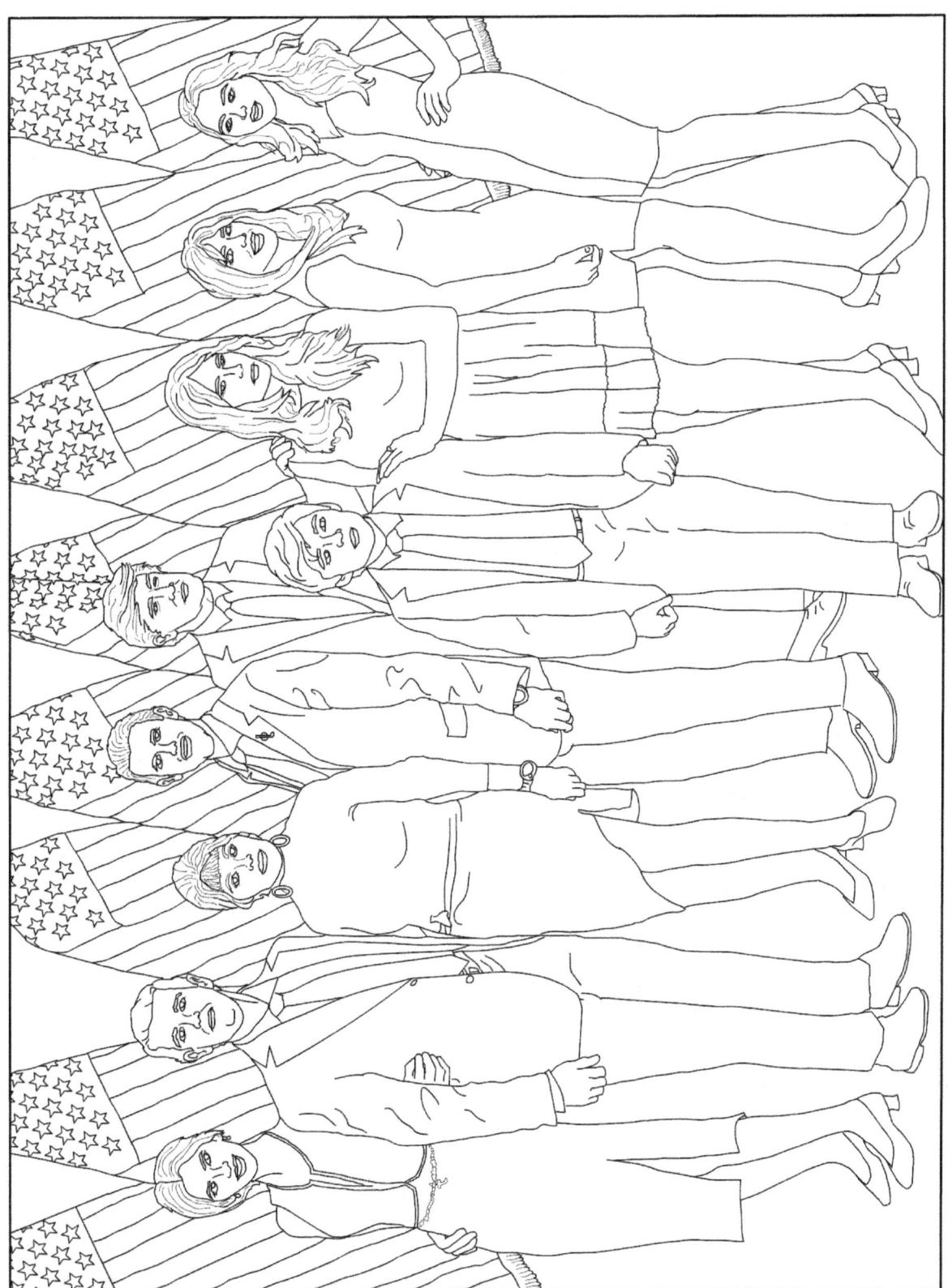

Entire Trump family including all 3 of the mothers of his children

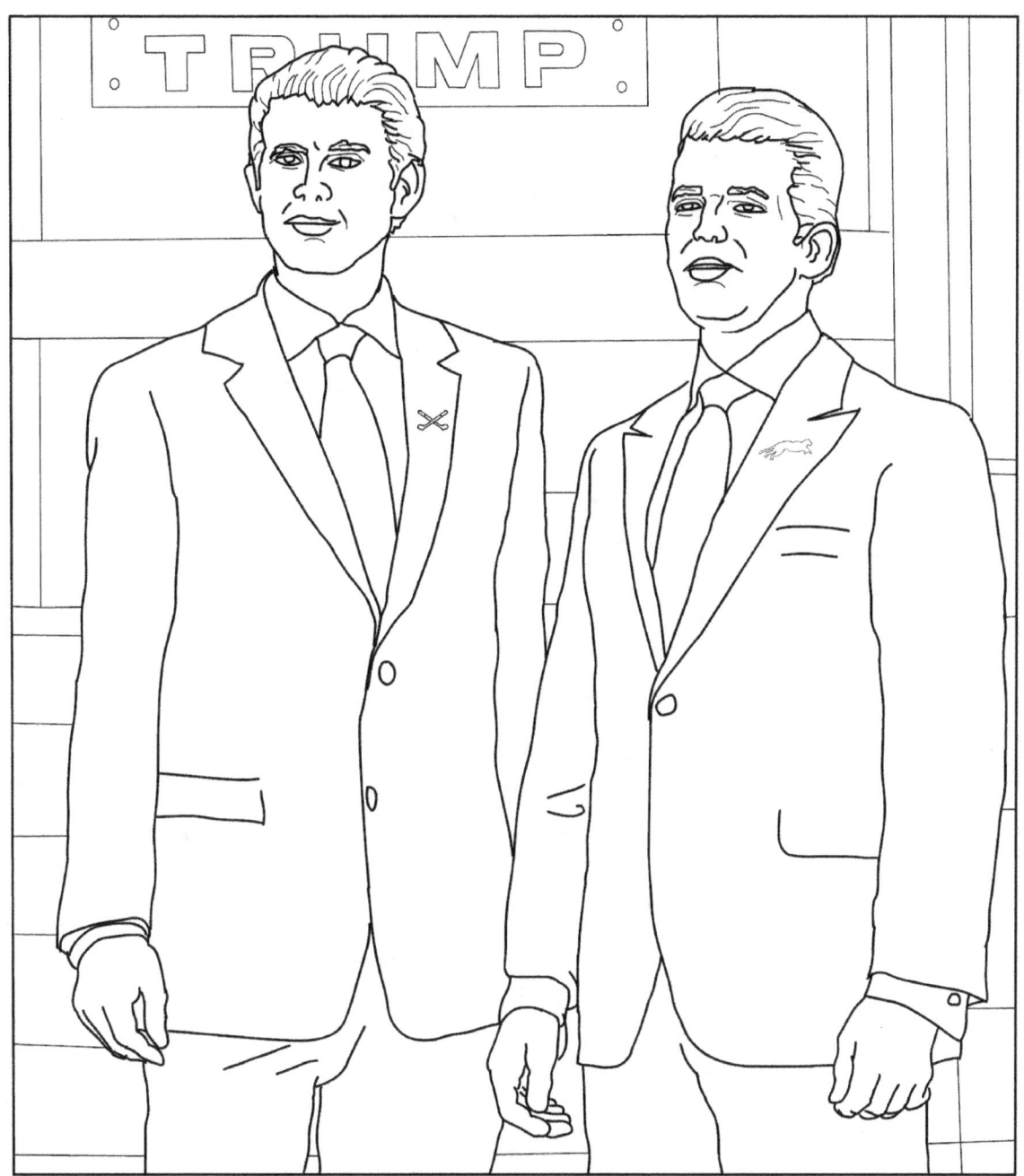

Eric trump (left) and Donald Jr.

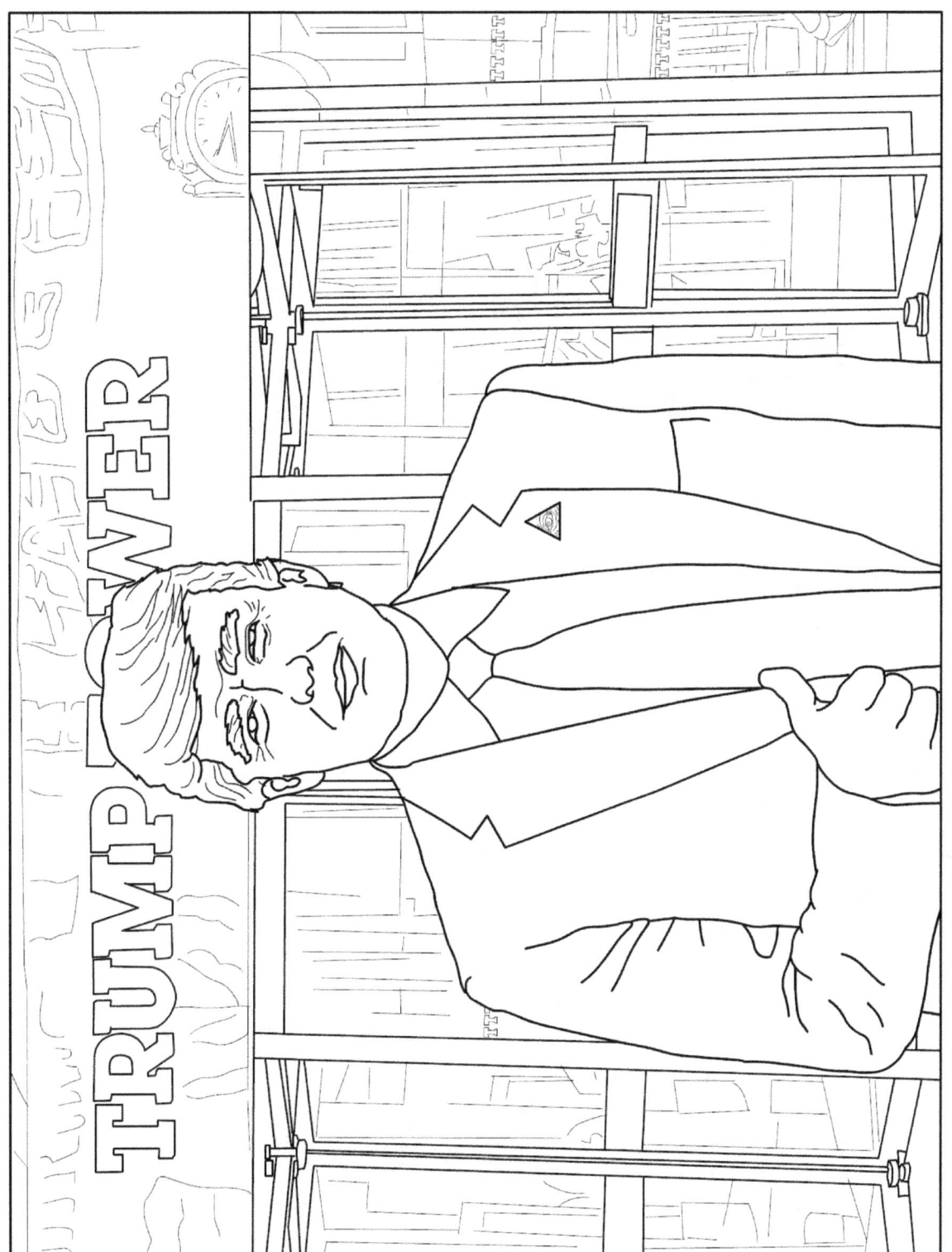

President Donald Trump is always a businessman

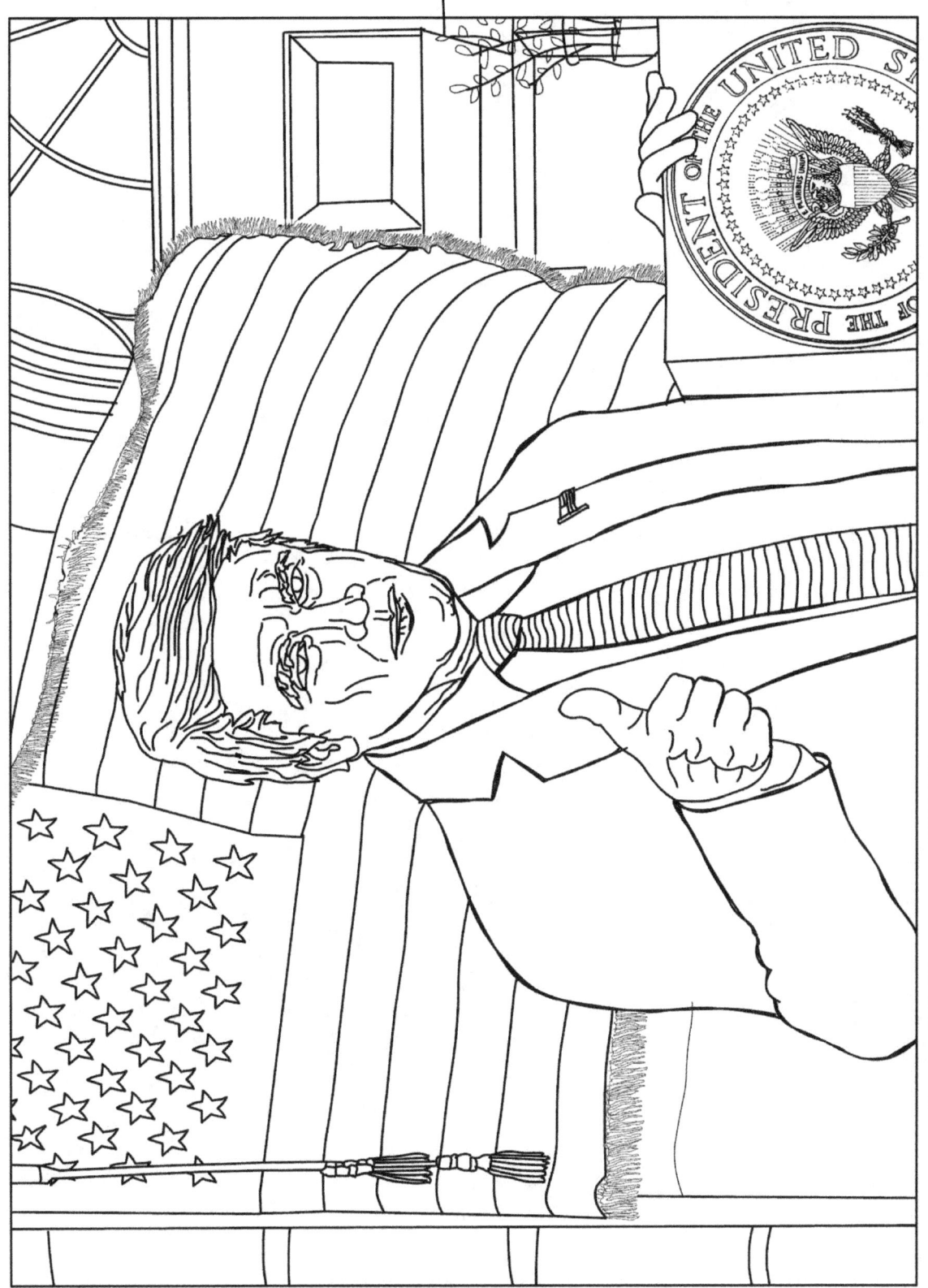

Donald Trump, 45th President of the United States

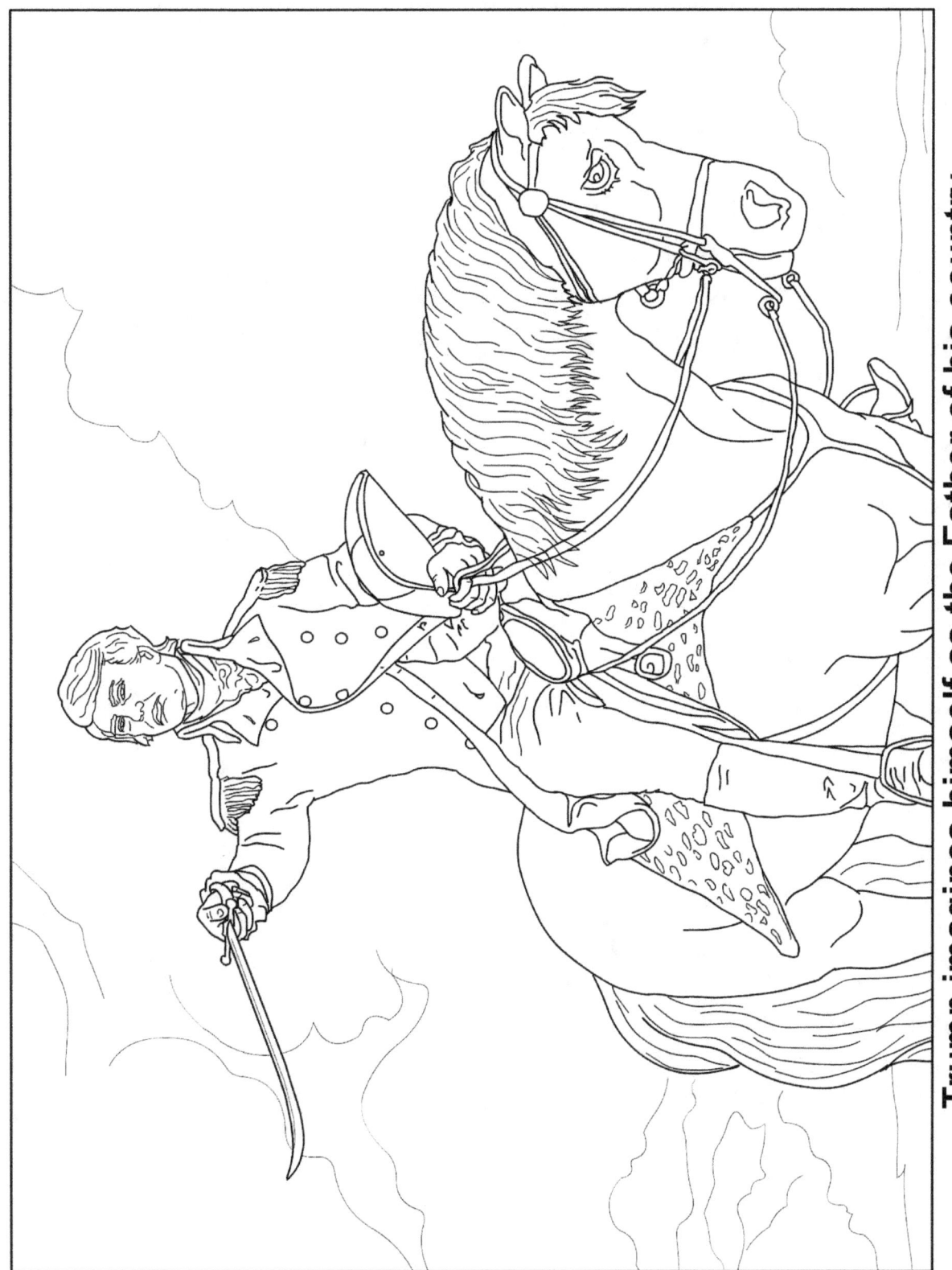

Trump imagines himself as the Father of his country

These portraits are by the Hawaiian artist Stephen E Jorgensen. He has over 200 other works of beautiful Hawaiian art available on his Etsy website. Most of his work is large canvas wall hangings, some of which are reduced to coloring pages in his other coloring books. See these at hawaiiseascapes.etsy.com. Message the artist at his site listed above if you are interested in a full-sized original giclee stretched canvas painting of any of these Trump portrait paintings for your wall.

Check out my other books at Amazon. I have these books currently published:

Creation of the Universe and Other Strange Mormon Beliefs Revealed. (A church member tells all the Secrets the Authorities Don't Want to Talk About.)

How to Import From China Starting With $250 and Make a Small Fortune!

How To Use Your Money Making Genes to Become a Success and Make a Small Fortune.

How to Publish Books on Amazon Kindle and Make a Small Fortune, The E-Book Money Making System

Relaxing Hawaiian Scenes, An Adult Coloring Book (first in the series)

Relaxing Hawaiian Scenes II, An Adult Coloring Book (second in the series)

Thanks....

Short bios for each of Pres Trump's family members.

Pres. Donald J Trump: Born June 14, 1946. As a young man and with a loan of a million dollars from his father, Fred, Donald bought the Commodore Hotel in 1976 and renamed it the Grand Hyat, then by building his name into a brand name for properties around the world, he has managed to develop a net worth of around 3.7 billion USD.

Ivana Trump: Born in Czechoslovakia February 20, 1949, she was a fashion model when she met Donald Trump in NewYork, they they were married from 1977–1992. Ivana worked closely with Donald as the Vice President of Interior Design and managed many of his properties. They had 3 children, Donald Trump Jr. and Ivanka and Eric. However the Donald started fooling around with younger actress, Marla Maples and Ivana divorced him in 1992.

Marla Maples: Born October 27, 1963 in Georgia, she is an actress and television personality. Donald met Marla at a tennis tournament and they started seeing each other although he was still married to Ivana who had to send private detectives to try to keep track of him. After Ivana divorced Donald, he continued with Marla 2 years before marrying her shortly after she had his daughter Tiffany. They were married from 1993–1999, much of it unhappy as Marla discovered she couldn't change him in the slightest.

Melania Trump: Born April 26, 1970 in Novo Mesto, Slovenia. She was attending a university in Slovenia studying design and architecture when she left to become a model, which involved some shoots in the US, where she became a naturalized citizen. Melania started dating Donald Trump after meeting him at a Fashion Week party in New York City in September 1998 while the Marla Maples divorce was being finalized, and married him in 2005 and then gave birth to their son, Barron, the following year.

Donald Trump Jr: Born December 31, 1977 in New York City, NY. His mother Ivana, sent her children to boarding schools to keep them away from the problems developing with her marriage to Donald Trump. Donald Jr. attended University of Pennsylvania's Wharton School, where he gained a B.S. degree in Economics, is an active vice-president in the Trump organization and with his brother Eric will manage the business while his father is President of the United States. Married to wife Vanessa in 2005. 5 children.

Ivanka Trump: Born October 30, 1981 in New York City, NY. She attended a boarding school. Then went on to Wharton Business School at the University of Pennsylvania, from which she graduated cum laude with a bachelor's degree in economics in 2004. She is the executive vice-president of the Trump Organization, and runs her own sub-brand of fashion clothing and jewelry, and is a former reality TV personality, as well as an author and fashion model. She is the 2nd child and daughter of U.S. President Donald Trump and his first wife Ivana Trump. Married to Jared Kushner, 2009, has 3 children.

Eric Trump: Born January 6, 1984 He went to a boarding school, then he graduated with a degree in finance and management, with honors, from Georgetown University. He now serves as a trustee of The Trump Organization, and was a longtime Executive VP in the company. He is the third child and second son of the President of the United States, Donald Trump, and Ivana Trump. Married Lara Yunaska in 2014. No children, but they have a dog, a beagle named Charlie.

Tiffany Trump: Born on October 13, 1993 Florida. She is the only child of Marla Maples and Donald Trump. Went to school in California where her mother went to get away from the publicity of the Trump name in New York. She graduated from the University of Pennsylvania, with a double-major in sociology and urban studies. She is considering a music career and perhaps a bit of modeling.

Barron Trump: Born March 20, 2006. Attends a private school in New York, and will not move to Washington DC and the White House for a while due to school. Likes to wear business suits like his father, his mother Melania calls him little Donald because he takes after his dad so much.

www.ingramcontent.com/pod-product-compliance
Lightning Source LLC
Chambersburg PA
CBHW081857170526
45167CB00007B/3051